FOUR SIGHT

FOUR SIGHT

The Essential Steps to Optimize
and Grow Your Optometry Practice

DR. LAMONT BUNYON

purposely
created
PUBLISHING

FOURSIGHT

Published by Purposely Created Publishing Group™

Copyright © 2019 Lamont Bunyon

Printed in the United States of America

ISBN: 978-1-64484-065-8

DEDICATION

I'm dedicating this book to my superhero mother, Madeline Bunyon, and my superhero father, Robert Bunyon, two of the most important and influential people in my life. They have been real superheroes for me since day one. If it were not for my wonderful, caring, giving and sacrificing parents, I would not be Dr. Lamont today. More importantly, I would not be the husband, father and citizen that I am. My mom and dad believed in me unconditionally and invested in me early on, giving me strong confidence in myself, academically and spiritually. They always emphasized education (my books) and faith (attending church and living as a Christian) as keys to succeeding and living the life of my dreams. When I got all A's in elementary school, I fondly remember them encouraging and celebrating me and proudly telling anyone and everyone in our neighborhood how smart I was, how I was a sharp thinker, and how successful I would be as an adult. As a child, I recall them pushing me to succeed and to dream of a future as a doctor. My parents were my first teachers, cheerleaders, coaches, and most importantly, believers in Dr. Lamont Bunyon. They set the highest standards for me and continually pushed me to reach them. They demonstrated and modeled a work and life balance for me to follow. My dad, Robert Bunyon, is the hardest working and most humble man I know to this day. His work day consisted of getting up daily at four a.m. five days a week to work as a waiter, maître d', and banquet manager to make ends meet for me, my older brother, Leroy, my older sister, Lisa, and my mom, Madeline. He often came home tired after a long day at work but still found time to fix anything and everything in house, make a model car with me, and have family dinner with all of us. My mom (the real superhero bigger than Superman, Spiderman, and all of the X-Men) was a dedicated and caring leader in our home. She found time to do everything-make breakfast in the morning for all of us, ensure we were all properly and neatly dressed and on time daily for school and work every day. We all had perfect attendance throughout elementary and high school. Mom prepared our lunches, cleaned our home, cleaned all the clothes, prepare balanced dinner meals, assisted with homework, and gave us extra academic work she found for us to do. On top of it all, she worked as a substitute teacher and a part-time factory worker to support our family too. And do you want to know what my mom did the very best? My mom was the chief visionary for our family. She had a gift of foresight regarding what we could be if we did the right things in the right order. Looking back now and laughing out aloud, mom was really the first optometrist in our family and lives. She helped my family members clearly see future success, and she envisioned our success before we saw it. From day one, she proclaimed that all of her children would find success in life and at work. My parents' hard work and foresight produced three fruitful children.

Leroy, my brother, holds a bachelor's degree from Penn State and an MBA from St. Joseph's University. He is a marine, an auditor, a wonderful husband, supportive father, and dedicated community volunteer leader with Alpha Phi Alpha Fraternity and the Prince Hall Masons.

Lisa, my sister, has a bachelor's degree and an MBA from Howard University. She is a corporate executive, overseeing million dollar accounts, and the most driven and successful person I know. Lisa is also a loving aunt, daughter, and dedicated community volunteer leader with Alpha Kappa Alpha Sorority and the Eastern Stars.

Then there's me, Dr. Lamont, who holds a bachelor's degree from Hampton University and a doctorate in optometry from the New England College of Optometry. I am a father, husband, entrepreneur, business coach, and dedicated volunteer leader with Alpha Phi Alpha Fraternity, 100 Black Men of America, The National Optometric Association, The Maryland Optometric Association, and other organizations.

My greatest thanks go to my favorite optometrist and the best doctor I know, Dr. Mesheca Carter Bunyon. Thank you a million times plus to my best friend, my confidante, my first lady, and my wonderful wife, Mesheca! I am your partner in this life, and I am blessed to have all of your love and support. Thanks goes out a million more times to the two brightest and most beautiful lights of my life, my super sons, Micah and Madden! Thank you both for giving me a reason to smile each and every day and for the privilege of being your father. My greatest wish is to do as good a job with you as my parents did with me.

Thank you to my Medical Moguls family, 100 Black Men family, Hampton Alumni family, Four Brown Eyes Optometry family, and my Alpha Phi Alpha Fraternity brothers for the inspiration and support.

Finally, thank you to anyone reading this manuscript. It is my hope that you are as inspired to optimize what is next in your life as I was to write this book.

TABLE OF CONTENTS

INTRODUCTION

Congratulations for reading *FourSight: Four Steps to Optimize Your Optometry Practice*. This book will provide a roadmap for starting an optometry practice. A problem for many young optometrists is that there is no readily available resources addressing the raw, true story of what happens when everything goes wrong in opening your optometry practice and what to do next. This book will teach you how to create a vision plan, a mindset plan, a business set up plan, and a plan for continued success for your optometry practice. This information will help doctors of optometry confidently launch and grow their practices in the proper manner the first time. The sooner you start working on the action steps in this book the sooner you will start building your dream business. Stop extending your problems and launch your own private optometry practice. Happy reading and get started today!

The goal of this book is to use common eye care terminology and tie in the meanings to the readers' personal and professional lives. Special emphasis will be given to the optometrists reading this book as a foundation for launching and growing their practices and lives.

My name is Dr. Lamont T. Bunyon (a.k.a. Dr. Lamont OD), and I am an award-winning optometrist, speaker, and consultant. In addition, I am a sought-after private practice expert, teaching optometrists how to launch and grow optometry practices, eye care clinics, and optical shops. I am an OPTOPRENEUR and a leading thinker in the area of community optometry care. I meet with doctors one-on-one and in groups, traveling the country to instruct and provide private practice advice to those in need.

I am so excited to be in my twentieth year of practicing as a doctor of optometry. I graduated from the New England College of Optometry as an award-winning student and leader, serving on the New England College of Optometry Board of Trustees, the Massachusetts Optometry Society Board, and as Student President while at the college. I have served as a leader in the optometry profession as President of the Central Maryland Optometric Society, first Vice President of the Maryland Optometric Association, Secretary of the National Optometric Association, Treasurer of the National Optometric Association, and founder of the Four Brown Eyes social media group, the largest online community of African-American doctors of optometry and optometry students. I have been recognized as a top doctor, winning the Maryland Optometrist of the Year and being a doctor, leader, member, and speaker with corporate groups such as IDOC, Vision Source, and Transitions Optical. I built a private practice cold, and now, fourteen years later, I have a business model that earns millions of dollars annually and serves the community with many free and charitable works. I have faithfully served 50,000 people in my predominately African-American community in Greater Washington, DC and Prince Georges County, Maryland, where I am known for delivering professional vision care with a personal touch. Over a three-year period, I envision my business helping one hundred doctors of optometry successfully launch their optometry businesses while having time for their families and communities.

Dr. Lamont's Story

Let me share the other part of my story, the realest part of my story, the story that kept me up at night and that pushes me to work harder. My first private practice in optometry failed. I spent years planning every detail. I found the perfect community. I was in a dream location, surrounded by educated and wealthy residents in a desirable suburban community right outside of Washington, DC. I had the perfect partner, a kindly, older optician, who knew all the ins and outs of the optical business and was a great friend and confidant. We had all of the best equipment, all the hottest designer eyewear, and were opening with an enthusiastic clientele who were ready for our services. We had our grand opening, and it was a glorious day of new patients, eyewear sales, happy smiles, proud owners, and workers. I did it. I achieved my American dream! I made it as a doctor and as a business owner. I launched my dream practice, and everything was going to be great.

I lost everything to grand theft one week after I opened my doors for the grand opening. Can you imagine walking into your brand-new business and seeing your items missing and in disarray? My partner encouraged me to stay the course and plan to reopen. I honestly did not know what to believe or hope for at that time. A week later, we reopened the business. Days later, we were robbed again, and everything was stolen plus office equipment this time. I still remember the broken glass, the stench of fingerprint dust all over my brand-new office, detectives all over my office, the feeling of walking on broken glass everywhere, and the missing eyeglasses and equipment. I used all of my personal savings to buy every piece of equipment and all the high-priced designer eyewear…now all gone. I had to close my doors and end my dream. I had to rebuild and go from *entrepreneur* to *employee* again. I explained to my wife and family that all was lost, and I did not know what to do. I went from the best time of my life to the worst time of my life and was broke in less than two weeks. What do I do now?

I scaled back my expenses. I filed my insurance claims. Thankfully, I got out of my three-year lease with the property manager. I dissolved my relationship with my optician partner. I went back to working part-time in corporate optometry and private practice employee optometry.

Here is the good news from the dark story I just shared. I reopened in a new location six months later. I scaled back even more. I worked even more part-time jobs to support the new office. I did not pay myself for two years, so I could slowly build my private practice back and more importantly, my dream back. This all happened in 2005, fourteen years ago. For the past twelve years, I've built the optometry practice business of my dreams. I pay myself just as much as I would make if I was working for someone else's business. I have free time to volunteer in the community weekly, mentoring and coaching young people over ten hours a week. I run a private optometry practice that is thriving in the market and delivers professional vision care with a personal touch to thousands of patients every year. Now, I want to share the how and the why and the what to do with other doctors of optometry and motivate them to succeed even when they have a cataclysmic business setback.

My mother, Madeline, gave me this Bible verse to live by as a young teen, and it has been one that has supported me throughout my private practice business journey. It's Psalm 30:5, King James Version. "For his anger endureth but a moment; in his favour is life: weeping may endure for a night but, joy cometh in the morning."

Chapter One

FAR-SIGHTEDNESS (HYPEROPIA)
VISION FOR YOUR PRACTICE

hyperopia
  noun
hy·per·opia | \ ˌhī-pə-ˈrō-pē-ə \

Definition of *hyperopia*

The online version of the Merriam Webster Dictionary defines hyperopia as "a condition in which visual images come to a focus behind the retina of the eye and vision is better for distant than for near objects." It is also known as "farsightedness."

Farsightedness or hyperopia is one of the most common visual disorders affecting people. Patients may complain of cloudy or foggy vision (blur), headaches above their brow, eye pain (astenopia), or eyes getting tired when focusing from distance to near (accommodation). Additionally, a patient's complaints may include losing their place and double vision (diplopia) when reading at near. Farsightedness or hyperopia is treated with prescription, specifically curved lenses that will focus the patient's vision clearly and comfortably. Your doctor of optometry will use a retinoscope, a handheld tool that shines light into your eye and perform a spectacle refraction with a lens rack or phoropter machine, changing lenses while asking you if the letters look better or worse to determine your lens prescription. The doctor is taking time to find the correctly powered lenses to accurately focus images onto your retina. Plus-powered, prescribed lenses will magnify the image, providing sharp vision when the patient is wearing the eyeglasses or contact lenses. The correct plus-powered lens prescription will correct your farsightedness or hyperopia.

In life, having farsightedness is a great asset when planning your future steps. It helps to be able to magnify what you are dreaming and aspiring to achieve.

I grew up in a middle-class home in the West Oak Lane section of Philadelphia, Pennsylvania. My earliest passion was drawing and writing about superheroes from comic books. I loved to create my own stories and characters. My favorite original characters were Strong Man, Fast Forward, and an African-American superhero police family called The Heat. The characters represented traits I valued highly as a child: personal or mental strength, fast forward or future planning, and personal and community accountability. I spent countless hours tweaking my own superhero creations and incorporating my academic love of science, history, and math into their stories. My mother worked as a substitute teacher for children with special needs in the Philadelphia Public School System. Mom would often come home and take time to have long conversations with me about my future and what I should focus on to serve others and provide a life for myself. At eleven-years-old, after a conversation with my mother, she suggested that I become a doctor. My mother, Madeline, believed I was highly intelligent and gifted in understanding science. She recognized that I cared about others, so she thought becoming a doctor would be a great career for me. I was (and still am) a "momma's boy." I valued what she said and decided this was a solid and attainable goal. We agreed on a plan that would take another fifteen years to become reality. My mom and I started my farsighted plan of one day becoming a doctor. We were soon joined by my supportive father, older brother, older sister, and countless other people in my community. Each year, we focused on this goal of me graduating one day as a doctor. I reminded myself on a regular basis that I was going to be doctor, and I was also reminded by everyone else too. I was now focused on helping my community as Doctor Lamont one day.

To help keep my focus on this farsighted plan of becoming a doctor, I had to study very hard in school. I was a straight A student at my elementary school, St. Athanasius in West Oak Lane, and avoided things that could distract me from my academics. I went to the top public high school, Central High School. I worked harder than ever in high school to keep up with the smartest and sharpest, young minds in Philadelphia. I graduated from Central High School and went off to one of the most highly regarded historically black colleges and universities in the United States, Hampton University in Hampton, Virginia. At Hampton University, I majored in biology/premed while working as a waiter to support myself throughout college. I finished Hampton University and went on to one of the oldest and most prestigious optometry institutions in the United States, the New England College of Optometry in Boston, Massachusetts. I filled the last slot in my optometry class of 1999 after proving myself to the admissions professors, following an intense, rigorous summer program competing with other students. Optometry school was the most difficult and challenging period of my young life. I had to study ten hours daily along with practicing clinical exam procedures for four years. Finally, in May 1999, fifteen years from that fateful conversation with my mother, countless hours of academic and clinical work, plus the ups and downs of young adult life, I graduated as Dr. Lamont Tyler Bunyon! My dream came true, I was fulfilled and happy and my mom even more so! I achieved my farsighted (hyperopia) plan of becoming a doctor. So what did I do next? After graduating from optometry school, I launched my next farsighted vision plan, opening up a private optometry practice serving my community.

Optometry and Life Lesson Learned:

Envision your success and make up your mind to succeed in your practice. Get the right prescription (plan) for your farsightedness (hyperopia) and use it. Find the right doctor, coach, parent, or mentor to help you achieve your goals.

Visualization Time Strategy: Saving your time, saving your money.

FIRST STEP: VISUALIZATION

Visualize what your optometry practice will look like.

Visualization Pie in the Sky Strategy: Create a vision board. Include everything you see and want in your ideal practice in pictures.

You have to first visualize what you want your dream practice to be before you can achieve and fulfill all of your dreams.

Do you want a large, futuristic office with all the latest bells and whistles?

Do you want a family-friendly practice that is the staple of your community?

Do you want to be the doctor with a niche practice that caters to a specific community epidemic or answers the call for evidence-based treatment and care?

Do you want to return to the days when you listened to your patients intently and learned empathically what was wrong and how to heal them?

Do you want a million-dollar practice with a high demand of patients and an exclusive community that you serve?

What is your vision of the practice that will answer your burning desire to serve others?

What does an optimized optometry practice look like to you? What doesn't it look like?

SECOND STEP: MODELING

Visualize and find models and mentors to focus on.

I chose to have a patient-focused, family practice in a community similar to the community I grew up in Philadelphia.

When I was growing up in Philadelphia, I was greatly influenced to become a doctor by two community doctors in the West Oak Lane/East Germantown section of Philadelphia where I lived. One of the doctors was Dr. Dasen, a dentist, who had a practice in a row home on Ogontz Avenue. He saw his dental patients on the lower level of his home. Dr. Dasen was the doctor who would come downstairs from his row home and take time to care for anyone who needed dental care. He was not about insurance or million-dollar smiles, but instead, he was about caring for the patients in his community and educating them about their dental health. He was a highly respected doctor who listened to his patients and knew all the members of families intimately. He didn't only know about their teeth but about them too. Dr. Dasen made my visits to the dentist less scary, was always caring, and put me at ease even when he used the dental drill or removed a cavity.

The other doctor who greatly influenced me was Dr. Jerome, a Caribbean doctor who also practiced in a corner row home and had a heart of gold. Dr Jerome would have ten to twenty patients in his waiting room who he would patiently give the utmost attention regarding their medical and personal care. Dr. Jerome would do everything! He could do minor surgeries and always had a sample bottle of whatever medication you needed on the spot. If my mother, Madeline, showed up with one of us needing medical care, he would take what seemed like all the time in the world to care for us and all of our needs. I would often marvel at how he answered questions and concerns over and over again to care for all of my family. He cared for the bee sting I had on my upper eyelid, my mother's aging woman issues, my dad's bad feet, my sister's pain concern, and my brother's concern about his muscles. He accepted whatever copay amount my parents could afford and was always willing to take a payment on the next payday. He loved our family. He respected our family. He cared for our family, and we and all of our community loved, cared, and respected him too. It was never about copay or reimbursement amounts. It was always about how he could make us feel better, be better, and be healthier. Dr. Jerome took time to focus like a laser. I cannot recall going to Dr. Jerome once and not feeling that he had fixed me or my family and made us better. These doctors, Dr. Dasen and Dr. Jerome, these great men, shaped the reasons I wanted to be a doctor and to have a practice in a community that I lived in. They shaped my dream practice that I have today. Do you want a dream practice to serve others?

THIRD STEP: OFFICE STAFF

Visualize and get the right team.

Visualize what the dream staff will be like and what they will do for your practice. To have the dream practice you also must have the dream staff. Write down the exact skills and personality qualities that you are looking for in your employees. You have to find and then cultivate the right people in your practice who will listen to you and most important-ly, to your patients. You need caring staff who are dedicated professionals, who are driven by the pur-pose of your office and not just a paycheck. Your selection of staff members is the ultimate driver to your practice dream coming to fruition. I discov-ered, over the years, that the personal investment you make early on in your staff's professional devel-opment will yield the biggest return on investment in your office. Your staff will make or break your office! Remember, they are the first smile someone sees and the first voice they will hear when they en-ter your office. They will set the tone for the en-tire visit and influence what a patient experiences in your practice. They will know all the intimate de-tails of your office and all about all of your patients. They will know how much money you make and how much you spend. They will have to faithfully and honestly collect your copays, file your claims, handle insurance company inquiries, maintain office inventory, and answer every fax and every phone call that comes into your office. You need to keep them in the right mindset and incentivized for their own growth. They should always feel like they are valuable and loved by you. One pearl you can never neglect is thanking them regularly for all that they do because they are the leading assets driving your practice's success in profit, purpose, and legacy.

FOURTH STEP: PATIENT COMMUNITY

Visualize and attract the community you want to serve.

Visualize the ideal patients you are best-suited to help. To have the dream practice, we already discussed that you must visualize it and the staff you need. Now, you must have the most important outside driver for your office's success. You need the dream community of patients attracted to and coming back again and again to your practice. You must cultivate these patients with expert clinical care, fair business practices, and love and nurturing. You have to provide a healthcare service that is second to none. Your practice should make every patient feel as if they are a king, a queen, a prince, or a princess. They must leave your practice wowed that what they received in healthcare was so great and so awesome that they advocate to their spouses, their kids, the rest of their family and friends, strangers, and even to people they do not like. You need patients bragging about how wonderful you are as a person, a clinician, and as a practice owner. You have to impress them to no end. To get your dream patients, you have to invest in knowing who they are, what they like, answer their health concerns, making it all about them first. It may not always simply be the sickness or ailment that is bothering them. From experience, I realize that I solve my patients' problems quickly and spend the rest of the time educating them about how to care for their eyes and prevent other problems from developing. I treat or prescribe eyeglasses, contact lenses, or eye-drops for my patients. The most important thing my practice provides is a comfortable environment, allowing them to be themselves during the time set aside for their exam. It is not about the patients' ability or capacity to pay but about how you can care for them and solve their problems. Your dream patients exist because you invest in them. You make them an enthusiastic investor in their own health-care, in themselves, and in your practice. The dream patient starts with your personal and professional treatment and becoming the doctor who treats them better than any other doctor ever has.

Homework

FARSIGHTED VISION + PASSION = PLAN

1. What is your vision?

_____
_____
_____
_____
_____
_____
_____
_____
_____
_____
_____
_____
_____
_____
_____
_____
_____
_____
_____

2. What will you do (passion) to reach your vision?

_____

_____

_____

_____

_____

_____

_____

_____

_____

_____

_____

_____

_____

_____

_____

_____

_____

_____

_____

_____

_____

_____

_____

_____

_____

3. What is your plan?

_____

_____

_____

_____

_____

_____

_____

_____

_____

_____

_____

_____

_____

_____

_____

_____

_____

_____

_____

_____

_____

_____

_____

_____

_____

Chapter Two

NEAR-SIGHTEDNESS (MYOPIA) MINDSET FOR YOUR PRACTICE

P D C

L P E D

P E C F D

E D F C Z P

F E L O P Z D

myopia
   noun
my·o·pia | \ mī-ˈō-pē-ə \

Definition of *myopia*

According to the online version of the Merriam Webster Dictionary, myopia is "a condition in which the visual images come to a focus in front of the retina of the eye resulting especially in defective vision of distant objects, or it can be defined as a lack of foresight or discernment."

Myopia is one of the most common vision conditions that patients present to eye care practitioners. Patients will often complain of squinting, blurry vision at a distance, and headaches. Use of minus-powered prescription eyeglasses or contact lenses will sharpen their vision by reducing the distance blur.

In life having nearsightedness is a great asset when planning future steps. It helps to be able to reduce and sharpen the view of what you are dreaming and aspiring to achieve. As an elementary and high school student, I distanced myself from distractions that took my eyes off of my long-term goal of becoming a doctor. I allowed myself to stay on a very narrow road to reach my academic achievements.

As a youth growing up in the 1980s in Philadelphia, I was exposed to many negative things including alcohol abuse, drug abuse, violence, and bad role models. I watched many young people make wrong choices that led to substance abuse, unemployment, incarceration, early pregnancies, and broken families. My parents were strong, positive role models, who consistently advised me to stay away from certain people and certain activities. I adopted this practice in my neighborhood and at school to avoid falling prey to peer pressure which may have led to bad decisions. I also adopted this mindset while pursuing my college degrees and establishing my private practice. I used a "myopia mindset" to stay focused on the things that matter most and to ignore the distractions from people and things.

Optometry and Life Lesson Learned:

Establish your mindset; keep your mind focused on positive things and people to support your goal. To develop your dream life or practice, you have to keep your mind set on positive thoughts. Seek out the right advisor, coach, or mentor to keep you encouraged.

STEP ONE: DAILY MINDSET

Practice daily affirmations.

One thing you can do to support your dream in-cludes reciting daily positive affirmations. You should recite the reasons you are a doctor. You should recite the reasons you want to heal others. You should recite the reasons you want to serve your community as a healthcare provider. You should re-cite the reasons you think you are the best at do-ing your practice. You should state the reasons your practice is different and unique. You should state the bold promise your practice will offer to others. You should state the reasons patients want to be a patient in your practice. You should state what you will do differently than any other doctor for them. Daily affirmations should be practiced every day at the same time, preferably in the morning when you first wake up. You should say them aloud in front of a mirror and declare them to your family in the mornings. Additionally, you should share your daily affirmation with the community via your website, social media, or email. You want everyone to know your daily affirmations in order to effect positive changes in the world.

STEP TWO: READ THE RIGHT THINGS DAILY

Make reading a daily habit.

It is important to read positive writings and books daily. You should make it a point to read twenty pages daily from empowering books about success, poems with positive energy, and journals. The texts should include enriching stories about people's lives and passions. To develop the right mindset for building your dream practice, you must feed your mind each day with the best written down thoughts. This daily ritual will open up your mind to seek others' thoughts and insight. This daily ritual will encourage your mind to listen and hear others before you go with your first thought. This daily ritual will promote lifelong learning through the wisdom of others' successes and failures. Reading is the leading way to open your eyes to the possibilities around you and keep your mind off of limitations as you pursue your dream practice. Your aim should be to complete at least one or two books monthly, review the daily news stories regarding your community, and subscribe to journals whose stories center around the development of an optometry practice.

STEP THREE: DAILY PHYSICAL ACTIVITY TO CLEAR YOUR MIND

Engage in physical activity daily.

Your day should also involve getting daily physical activity in to clear your mind. A twenty-minute walk will invigorate you physically and mentally. The fresh air will help clear your mind from toxic thoughts or energy and open your mind to the brilliance of a new day instead. I am astonished at how beautiful everything is as I walk in the mornings. Find a companion to walk with to enhance this physical activity. The partner may be your neighbor, your spouse, a friend, or a family member who will keep the energy positive and will hold you accountable. Commit to the same time daily and reward yourself when you have completed each walk. Daily physical activity promotes positive energy and fuels your mind with strategies for developing your dream practice.

STEP FOUR: DEVELOP YOUR FAITH BASE

Develop a spiritual life.

It is important to maintain a faith-based, purpose-filled life. Whether you subscribe to Christianity, another religion, or just lead a spiritual life, you need to have an awareness that the world is bigger than you. You should acknowledge that your purpose in life is more than money or good times. You should know that your passion for serving others as a healthcare provider is more than you. Maintaining this area of your life will require regular prayer or meditation, private and public gathering with other faith-based believers, and time devoted to growing your faith-based, purpose-filled life. During this time, you will develop critical skills in dealing with those who need your services and appreciate how

fortunate you are to be in a position to help someone else. You will need to find a way to give back to
your community in service. I volunteer each week
with the 100 Black Men of America, mentoring at-
risk youth. This weekly community service helps
these young men by giving them a positive example and energizes me to fuel my dreams from their
energy. You want to grow as a person, a doctor, an
entrepreneur, a parent, and a spouse by serving your
community. Let your example of success be seen and
shared with those less fortunate than you. You will
watch yourself stretch and grow in ways you have
never seen before. Most importantly, as your faith
grows, your mind will grow and bring your dream
into reality.

STEP FIVE: POSITIVE ENERGY SHARED

Give of yourself in a positive way.

Give positive comments and do positive things for
your friends and family. Commit to giving positive
energy and vibes to everyone you encounter every
day. Devote time to engaging everyone with a smile,
a compliment, and a warm greeting and goodbye.
This positive energy will be reciprocated as you deal
with patients, staff, and partners. You should never

underestimate how the positive energy you share can impact their lives. You may be the only person they receive this from. Practicing this daily will train you to convert positive or negative energy from patients into a positive experience. Remember, your dream practice will be built on the positive impression you leave on your patients during their visits and when they leave your office. I returned to Dr. Dasen and Dr. Jerome for the positive reinforcement and energy I received after every visit with them. I witnessed the impact it had on my mother and father every time they visited the office.

STEP SIX: LEARN TO LET GO OF THINGS HOLDING YOU BACK

Remove the obstacles.

To get your dream practice, you have to remove yourself from things that hold you back. This is another critical task. You must remove yourself from any distraction or deterrent that may keep you from building your dream practice. This may mean spending less time doing things you usually do. This may mean you have to separate yourself from your own tendencies that lead you away from investing in your dream practice. You have to focus like a laser on spending your free time and work time on building, building, and building your dream practice. You cannot waste any moments by being sidetracked or allowing your self-defeating, negative thoughts or emotions to take away your focus from your dream practice. Put your cellphone down, stop scrolling social media or watching internet videos, stop playing video games like Fortnight, and stop reading books not involved with building your dream practice. Instead, invest in reading textbooks or clinical journals, listen to podcasts, and converse with the top colleagues in your field. Network with the doctors who have the practice you want. Go to the convention and meet the million-dollar practice owners. Follow their social media community and posts, go to their lectures, and look at what they do in their free time to build their dream practices. To get your dream practice, you have to walk with other dream practitioners. You should allow yourself the freedom to ask them questions and find out what they did to build and succeed. Ask for their secrets to success and what they would do differently. Take action to achieve what they've achieved. Research why they chose their location, their community, the medical plans and hospitals they affiliate with, and the products they promote in their practices. Note what they sell specifically and why Know what they use as training resources. The secret is to remove yourself from things that do not promote your practice but stay engaged and focused on things that promote and build your dream business. This step cannot be underestimated. You must do like it says in the Bible regarding marriage; cleave to building your dream practice as if it was your spouse and leave your distractions behind. Remember you are building your dream practice!

Homework

NEARSIGHTED VISION (MINDSET) +
PASSION = PLAN

1. What do you need to focus your mind on first?

_____

_____

_____

_____

_____

_____

_____

_____

_____

_____

_____

_____

_____

_____

_____

_____

_____

_____

2. What do you have to limit (passion) to reach your vision?

_____

_____

_____

_____

_____

_____

_____

_____

_____

_____

_____

_____

_____

_____

_____

_____

_____

_____

_____

_____

3. What is your plan?

_____

_____

_____

_____

_____

_____

_____

_____

_____

_____

_____

_____

_____

_____

_____

_____

_____

_____

_____

_____

_____

_____

_____

_____

Chapter Three

DISTORTED VISION (ASTIGMATISM)
THE SETUP FOR YOUR PRACTICE

astigmatism
  noun

astig·ma·tism | \ ə-'stig-mə-ˌti-zəm \

The online version of the Merriam Webster Dictionary defines astigmatism as "a defect of an optical system (such as lens) causing rays from a point to fail to meet in a focal point resulting in a blurred and imperfect image or a distorted understanding suggestive of the blurred vision of an astigmatic person."

Astigmatism is another of the most common vision diagnoses and one of the top reasons patients come to see optometrists for correction. With astigmatism, you have blurry vision due to distortion of shape of your eye. Patients need lenses with cylinder power to correct the distortion and bring things into sharper focus.

In your practice, you need to correct several distortions while setting up your business. You need to properly set up your business as a business entity with the government. You need set up banking, payroll, and insurance services. You need to become a provider with medical insurance plans and market your business to attract patients. Most importantly, you must set up every office policy and procedure in writing to ensure that the same service is delivered consistently by your staff for your patients.

Early on in my practice, I suffered a severe business loss due to robbery and property damage. I was able to recover because I had invested in liability and business insurance that eventually paid for all of my business losses and lost wages. I did not take any shortcuts in setting up my business. I had to spend extra money to set up as a corporate business entity, but that saved me later on when the worst thing happened. Later on, as my business grew, another distortion developed with the employee culture. I had staff members who developed lazy habits and did not complete tasks. This resulted in disappointed patients, refunded money, missed payments, and in general, a sloppy business presentation. I had to establish an employee handbook and conduct training. I had to set business boundaries and learn to hire slowly and to fire quickly.

Optometry and Life Lesson Learned:

Set up your business properly and make sure you have the right resources and staff partners available to assist you. Take your time establishing these relationships, but if necessary, be prepared to terminate if they are no longer helpful to your practice. Seek out the right advisor, coach, or mentor to keep you encouraged.

STEP ONE: LEARN BUSINESS AND MONEY MATTERS

Get ready to begin before you open.

Here is an important lesson to learn. You are in business to be profitable, making money to support your life and grow your business. You have to make money. You have to have your purpose and passion anchored in making a profit. That is okay and necessary because people will come to your practice because of many things like locality, word of mouth, advertising, group connections, or personal history, but they will stay with you year after year because they value you and your practice. That factor has a monetary value on it, and it is okay to plan, project, and protect that too. You have to learn how businesses run. A successful business works from a low overhead (You do not spend too much.) and a high return on investment (You make a profit on what you are selling.), whether it is eye examination services or eyeglass frames or lens products.

STEP TWO: LEARNING INSURANCE PARTNERS

Insurance plans are important.

Contact every insurance carrier, so they know where you are. Spend time completing insurance applications and gathering necessary documents to meet credentialing requirements. For an optometry practice, contact the local and national medical carriers for Medicare, Medicaid, Blue Cross Blue Shield, Aetna, Cigna, and TriCare. Additionally, seek out the larger unions in your area and sign up for their medical plans. For your optometry practice, contact the national vision care providers, Vision Service Plan, Spectera, Davis Vision, Vision Benefits of America, and EyeMed and sign up for their plans. Later on, you may decide you do not want to be associated with a particular plan but starting out it is good to become credentialed with all of the major plans. Many of your patients will be on these plans, and you have to be available to see them when they come into your office. The different insurance companies will have different requirements for your practice including equipment requirements, hours of availability, office protocols, and delivery times for eyeglasses. Also, you have to stay knowledgeable about reimbursement cycles and reconciling payments, so you or your staff have the information ready for audits if necessary. To start getting insurance contracts, you will need to process the different insurance contract applications by working with one of the credentialing agencies in your state, so they can acquire your educational and legal backgrounds.

STEP THREE: KNOW YOUR PROJECTED NUMBERS

Your numbers matter.

Know the financial and free time goals you want to reach. You have to know where you want to be financially in order to attain that goal. You must know your numbers. Remember your financial goal must be tracked on a regular basis. A regular basis includes a daily, weekly, monthly, quarterly, and a yearly goal. Remember a goal without a plan is just a wish. My goal was to be able to pay myself as much as I would earn as an employed doctor with the added benefit of time and life freedom. I decided early on that I wanted to arrive to my work place without concerns of a boss or another business' financial goals weighing me down. I wanted to be driven by my own financial goal. What is that financial goal? Your financial goal has to be on the high end of your optometry practices, enough to pay all of your bills, enough to pay your student loans, enough to save for your children's futures, and enough to save a minimum of six to twelve months in reserve in case of a rainy day. That means you must always stay focused reaching those goals. In plain words, if you are making a million dollars a year, then you must make a quarter of a million every three months. You have to hit certain numbers regularly and have your staff scheduled to hit this successfully. To get your time freedom goals you have to set aside the time needed to reach your goals and to have all of the time you need to get those goals. Plan around the times your patients want to come in, when your staff wants to be there, and when you still have time to make the basketball game and have a date night.

STEP FOUR: DEVELOP A MARKETING PLAN

Market your practice in local magazines, on the web, and on social media where your patients routinely visit. I would strongly recommend that you market in the local consumer health magazines, the suburban journals, and popular, local social media business groups. For example, in my area, I advertise in two health magazines and a local suburban magazine that is mailed to tens of thousands of community residents and is found in all of the other local doctors' offices as well. Advertising in magazines will put you in a position where folks see you with other credible, well-established doctors and feel that you are part of that same community. Social media is a platform that just about everybody uses every single day for entertainment and for education. You must become social media savvy. Establish accounts with Facebook, Instagram, Twitter, LinkedIn, and YouTube, so your patients are able to find you on their social media choice. They are able to see your ads, letting them know about your services. Don't market your services by price. If you market by the lowest price, you will lose to somebody offering an even lower price. Instead market yourself as the best service provider. It is a much better standpoint if someone is going for quality service because then they'll choose you for the services and not for the price. Market directly to your community by participating in events, doing community service, and mailing flyers and direct marketing letters. For example, in my practice, we participated with the local chamber of commerce annual meeting where we give out anti-reflective cleaning cloths and eyeglass cleaner bottles to attendees. By taking this small step, folks became aware of our optometry practice and our brand in our community. In addition, our practice volunteers at local elementary school vision screenings for children, checking for undiagnosed hyperopia, myopia, and astigmatism. We also do this to advertise our practice and to make the local teachers aware of signs and symptoms that they will notice in their students. This small bit of community service carries great influence in drawing new patients to your office. Take advantage of the bulk mailings from the post office or drop mail into area housing communities in mailboxes. We also leave our mailers at churches, local recreation centers, or small businesses that want to partner with us or cross promote each other.

STEP FIVE: CONTINGENCY PLANNING

Have a backup plan.

Anticipating success and preparing for the worse is key when you set up your practice. When I started my business, the worst thing that could happen happened. As I recounted earlier, one week after I opened my office, we were burglarized and somebody stole all of the designer eyeglasses. It was a huge loss of the projected revenue that we were hoping for. Six months later, I opened our new office in a new location that was more secure. I negotiated a better contract this time and started with a smaller space. We knew that we would be able to negotiate for a larger space in under a year because this time we were better prepared for worse case scenarios than the first time. Planning for success and preparing for the worst are the reasons we were able to not only survive but thrive even from the beginning. We kept a reserve fund ready as an emergency. We suffered a major setback in the practice during year ten when a broken water pipe caused immeasurable damage to our office, damaging all the carpeting as well as the furniture. Thankfully, we had the right insurance and were fully covered, so we were able to order new equipment and carry on. Are you ready to envision success and prepare for the worse? This is absolutely critical in order to survive and thrive in your new optometry practice from the start. Get business insurance, liability insurance, and malpractice insurance. Establish a retirement plan from day one, and if necessary, get a 401K and 529 plan for your children. Establish a key man policy in the event that you are unable to perform your role as the key man of your practice. A key man policy will provide insurance financially if you are unavailable to work in your practice due to disability or death. When you get your liability insurance, make sure you have enough coverage to cover your practice fully in the event of a lawsuit against you for a medical error. Be sure you have health insurance that is with a reputable healthcare company to cover your expenses for you and your family.

STEP SIX: FINANCING AND CONTRACTING

Take out a loan and use someone else's money.

One of the strongest pieces of advice I would give to anyone starting an optometry practice is to take out a loan from a bank. When I started my first practice, I chose to fund it myself and that was a very bad mistake. You should take advantage of your credit, your home ownership, and your credibility as a doctor to get a practice loan that you will slowly repay. You can build the practice of your dreams without exhausting your own personal savings. Finance the startup costs of your new practice, rental costs for six months, utilities for six months, salary costs for six months, and equipment costs for five years.

Doctors, take the time to negotiate a good contract with the location you choose for your practice. Do not sign a ten-year agreement, instead sign a shorter term agreement. I would recommend a three to five-year agreement to give you flexibility and also to prevent costs from being too high in the event that you need to change course and move.

STEP SEVEN: YOUR HEALTH MATTERS

Are you healthy?

Get your health together. Start working out and eating right now. You are all you've got. You have to eat balanced meals daily just like your mom said; eat your vegetables, your starches, and your carbohydrates. You are the most important part of your practice. You must maintain your physical and mental health by exercising daily. Avoid being lazy or a couch potato; get out, move, stretch, and make sure that your body is in good working order. You need to visit your doctor regularly, so he or she can make sure that you are at peak performance.

Homework

DISTORTED VISION (ASTIGMATISM) + PASSION = PLAN

1. What distortions do you have in your life?

_____

_____

_____

_____

_____

_____

_____

_____

_____

_____

_____

_____

_____

_____

_____

_____

_____

_____

_____

2. What can you do today to find help to correct (make plans) the distortion?

_____

_____

_____

_____

_____

_____

_____

_____

_____

_____

_____

_____

_____

_____

_____

_____

_____

_____

_____

_____

3. What is your plan?

_____

_____

_____

_____

_____

_____

_____

_____

_____

_____

_____

_____

_____

_____

_____

_____

_____

_____

_____

_____

_____

_____

Chapter Four

AGING VISION (PRESBYOPIA)
THE LEGACY FOR YOUR PRACTICE

presbyopia
 noun

pres·by·o·pia | \ 'prez-bē- ˌō-pē-ə, 'pres-\

The online version of the Merriam Webster Dictionary defines presbyopia as "a visual condition which becomes apparent especially in middle age and in which loss of elasticity of the lens of the eye causes defective accommodation and inability to focus sharply from near vision."

Presbyopia is one of the most common visual problems in people over the age of forty. As we age, the collagen inside the eye stiffens and loses flexibility. As a result, we are not able to change the shape of our internal lens inside our eyes and bring near objects into clear focus (accommodation). Optometrists will prescribe bifocal eyeglasses with additional magnification power to provide sharp vision at near for their patients. These lenses will allow clarity for focusing on reading and computer work.

Optometry and Life Lesson Learned:

Clear up distortions that are part of building your optometry practice and life. This will take extra time, but it is the soundest investment you can make to have business and personal peace of mind. Seek out the right advisor, coach, or mentor to keep you encouraged.

STEP ONE: BUILDING WITH THE END IN MIND

Your practice is part of your legacy.

You are building a legacy from the day that you open your doors. Ultimately, your practice may serve as an investment for your family, spouse and children, so they have another resource to be able to draw from financially. Protect your investment-pay yourself first by investing into your retirement plan. Money from every paycheck should be directed into a savings plan. Build a cash nest egg for six to eight months. Keep accurate records for expenses, income, and taxes. Know your expenses, so that the information is available for future sale of your practice or financing needs of your practice.

STEP TWO: PROTECT YOUR PRACTICE BRAND

Your brand represents you.

Protect your brand; you must nurture the reputation of your practice. Your reputation is your biggest asset. You have to guard your reputation and be willing to offset small financial losses, if necessary, in exchange for building a great brand reputation. Ultimately, you will be known by word of mouth, and in this day and age, by word on websites as well. Invest additional money to market via your website, social media sites, and online search engines. I make it a habit to thank all patients for choosing our practice when there are so many choices available, and I promise them that we will not let them down. You must always respect and exceed their expectations. My big, brand promise is delivering professional vision care with a personal touch. I want every patient to leave my office feeling as if they know me. I want to be more than just another doctor of optometry. I want them to feel the same way that I felt about Dr. Dasen and Dr. Jerome. I want patients to view my office as a community resource and as a part of their healthcare family.

CONCLUSION

Thank you for reading this book. The important takeaways for this book include establishing your practice vision, developing a positive mindset, preparing for a proper business set up, and keeping your practice legacy in mind from the start. The action steps to accomplish these goals include finding a mentor, hiring a business coach, and investing time in your health and business education immediately. These actions will benefit you by helping you start your business prepared for the best while being ready if the worst occurs.

ABOUT THE AUTHOR

Dr. Lamont Bunyon is an award-winning optometrist, speaker, and consultant. He is also a sought-after private practice expert who teaches optometrists how to launch and grow successful optometry practices, eye care clinics, and optical shops. In his spare time, he is a committed community service worker, who mentors youth and volunteers his expertise by doing free vision screenings. He believes in doing everything with excellence and delivers professional vision care with a personal touch.

Dr. Bunyon is an active member of Alpha Phi Alpha Fraternity, Inc., serving as President of the Sigma Alpha Lambda Chapter. In addition, he is an active member and Vice President of 100 Black Men of America, Prince Georges County Chapter.

He has been married to fellow optometrist, Dr. Mesheca Carter Bunyon, for fifteen years, and they have two sons, Micah and Madden. His hobbies are collecting comic books, public speaking, and coaching youth sports.

Learn more at
www.DrLamontOD.com

NOTES

NOTES

NOTES

NOTES

NOTES

NOTES

NOTES

NOTES

NOTES

NOTES

NOTES

NOTES

NOTES

NOTES

NOTES

NOTES

NOTES

NOTES

NOTES

NOTES

www.ingramcontent.com/pod-product-compliance
Lightning Source LLC
Chambersburg PA
CBHW071501210326
41597CB00018B/2639